DELIVERANCE FOR REAL
WORKBOOK

Dr. Shirley R. Brown, Th.D

DELIVERANCE FOR REAL WORKBOOK

DR. SHIRLEY R. BROWN, Th.D

Unless otherwise indicated, all scripture quotations are taken from the New Living Translation of the Bible.

DELIVERANCE FOR REAL

WORKBOOK

ISBN: **978-1-7372435-1-2**

© 2021 All rights reserved

Dr. Shirley R. Brown, Th.D

www.DestinyIntMinistries.org

No part of this book may be reproduced or transmitted in any form or by any means, electronic or mechanical, including photocopying, recording, or by any information storage and retrieval system, without permission in writing from the publisher.

All rights reserved.

TABLE CONTENTS

How to Use the Book and Workbook Together……………………………......2

Covenant Agreement……………………………………………………….3

Deliverance Minister……………………………………………………....5

Phase 1: Identity…………………………………………………………11

Phase 2: Demons and Demonic Legal Rights……………………………......21

Phase 3: Biblical Authority…………………………………………….....38

Phase 4: Inner Healing…………………………………………………..48

Phase 5: Rejection……………………………………………………......61

Phase 6: Spiritual Contamination………………………………………..70

Phase 7: Binding and Loosing…………………………………………….....81

Phase 8: Trauma………………………………………………………...93

HOW TO USE THE BOOK AND WORKBOOK TOGETHER

Deliverance For Real is designed to assist you with getting a clear understanding of who you are and how you may have been held up in your thoughts and emotions. It is an activation tool you can apply to strive to be free from all bondages and to assist others with the baggage of the past. The past does not dictate your future.

I desire that you will use the workbook with the book "Deliverance for Real" to begin your freedom walk. You will not just read and know a thing but you will read and experience a thing. That ultimate thing will be your freedom. Nothing prospers without work, so today begin your journey of work. Wake and declare you will be free and allow nothing to stop. Stopping will only delay and delay is not an option.

Dr. Shirley R. Brown, Th.D

Covenant agreement for "Deliverance for Real"

I, _____, agree to work diligently to be free of the chains that have bound me for too long and Dr. Shirley R. Brown will stand in agreement with me through prayer that this will be the start of my deliverance point. I will take the foundational principles and apply them. I will study the word, adhere to sound doctrine and hold myself accountable to my leadership. I am now ready to make this sound decision to be enlightened and equipped to walk in my God-ordained destiny. I will trust God and renounce all the past sins and negative words. I will be honest first and foremost with myself so I can be honest with God. Today is my declaration of receiving the best that God has for me.

Signature of Agreement: _____

DELIVERANCE MINISTER

What is Deliverance?

_____

_____

_____

What is a Deliverance Minister?

_____

_____

_____

    In serving the Lord in any capacity, especially as a deliverance minister, you will have a lot of personal sacrifices. I must tell you; this is not a popular ministry because it has been misleading by portraying that there is a lot of screaming. A whole lot of crazy stuff going on and that is not what it is. We can so easily take ourselves out of the will of the Lord by practicing cultic practices, not even knowing that is what we are doing. We can arrive at things so quickly in our minds and decide that is what we are supposed to do. However, the ministry of deliverance is to set the captives free. You can sit down and have a conversation and help someone get free and give hope to the hopeless. Everyone is called to the ministry of Jesus Christ; however, everyone may not operate in the fullness of it. So, again, the deliverance ministry is the ministry of Jesus.

List some of the acts of deliverance associated with the ministry of Jesus?

_____

_____

_____

Now, the deliverance minister first needs to be **free**, not perfect. Hear me good, you need to have been set free of your things. Always examine yourself, you want to examine the motives, even why you do a thing. As we assess our issues and our inner enemies, we get free. Then, we can be effective in what we do as far as deliverance ministry and helping others. The effectiveness comes when the minister understands his delegated authority. The Father gave us authority. He gave authority to His Son, and the Son has given authority to us. Acknowledge where the authority comes from. So, I say something simple, confess your mess and cast your demon out.

Have you ever asked yourself the question why do I do what I do? If so, what were your motives?

_____

_____

_____

Can you identify your inner enemies?

_____

_____

_____

I think if you are a minister, period, you should know the qualifications of ministry. You have got to be scripturally sound; I would say follow the model of Jesus in Mark 9:14-29 where Jesus did an interview process. He silenced the demon first and then He did His interview process.

Read Mark 9:14-29 and list the key points of deliverance found in the passage.

_____

_____

_____

You must overcome fear, you cannot do deliverance from a place of fear. You just cannot. You cannot allow the enemy to think that he is challenging you. Don't fear, the enemy has no control or power at all over you. There will be no fear of a demon and there will be no fear of man. The fear of man is criticism, rejection, and fear of what someone else is going to say about your ministry. Know who you are, what you stand for, and do not get yourself tied up in the spirit of legalism. Do what Christ said to do.

Read and write out the scripture 2 Timothy 1:7. What stands out to you in this scripture? _____

_____

_____

_____

Ministers of the gospel must always be cautious when preaching and teaching so that they do not enter witchcraft themselves. We can open doors ourselves. These are the doors we must be cautious of:
- Cannot use scripture to control people
- Cannot be rebellious
- Should not be argumentative
- Should not condemn one another
- Walk in the spirit of pride

We have got to learn to be free of blame and we have got to grab ahold of this at a different place. Are we ministers or are we practicing witchcraft? A witch doctor professes to heal or cure by some type of sorcery or some type of hex. In other words, he does what he does his way.

In reading this passage, have you opened one or more of these doors? If so, what was the result of the door being opened?

_____

_____

_____

We do not want to get into religious error. If you get in religious error, what you wind up doing is opening up more demonic doors, and so it's better sometimes to walk away, sit down, be quiet, and find out the whole matter of a thing. Learn not to move so quickly. Like I said, just learn to be still for a minute and listen.

What does Deliverance cost:

_____

Have you heard of these so-called deliverance ministers who give instructions, yet you always have to come back for additional assistance? If so what was your experience?

_____

_____

_____

Why would someone keep going back?

_____

_____

_____

The enemy will try any tactic and any trick to keep God's people from spiritual warfare.

What are the 3 areas of witchcraft? Where have you seen these spirits in operation?

_____

_____

_____

Were you able to identify them at the time?

_____

Read Acts 19:13-17 and summarize the passage. What trauma occurred from this event?

_____

_____

_____

_____

Areas a deliverance minister must foster:
- Energy is needed when preparing for a deliverance session. Sometimes it is long hours. Sometimes you can be up late at night.
- Keep yourself healthy. Eat properly
- Get proper rest
- Maintain a balanced lifestyle
- Must be able to compartmentalize issues
- Do not be offended by odors
- Have genuine compassion
- Confidentiality
- Strong prayer life
- Discernment

Read and write Mark 6:31. What does this scripture speak to you concerning rest?

_____

_____

_____

How important is rest to the believer?

_____

_____

_____

I want you to have the power of using the name of Jesus. I want you to understand that God has set us up for a time like this. We are going to go forth and set others free. Joel 2:25 KJV, *"And I will restore to you the years the locust has eaten the cankerworm and the caterpillar and the palmerworm my great army, which I sent among you."* Understand right there, that means everything that those years snatched away from you or you walked around depressed because of the situation, is about to be restored. But we must be a participant in it. We can no longer sit back and cry. Oh, woe is me. Oh, Jesus. The first lesson you learn as a deliverance minister, you do not go to God, begging and pleading. He has given us authority; He has given us information.

Prayer of Activation:

I pray God, the things that have been released to your servants, it does not fall to the ground. It becomes like a seed planted in them and they are going forward and understanding there is more of you to pour into them. So, Father, we come against the enemy and we let him know he will not snatch back anything they have learned. They are walking in their freedom; they will have their healing, and they will be able to do great and mighty exploits. And Father, I cancel the spirit of fear on those who have a desire, those that have cried out and said, I want to go forth, but I am so afraid. God, let them begin to rise and be the end-time ministers you have called them to be in the name of Jesus. And let it be so in Jesus' name.

Key Takeaways:

_____

_____

_____

_____

Phase One:
The Identity Phase

Our focal scripture is going to be Colossians 3:3 NLT, *"For you died to this life, and your real life is hidden with Christ in God."* Taking wisdom from the teaching of my spiritual father, Bishop George Bloomer, I recall him always saying to read a scripture above your focal scripture and maybe even two to three below. Reading the preceding verses will help you gain a clearer understanding.

Read and write Colossians 3:2-3 and list key points that address identity.

_____

_____

_____

Define identity:

_____

_____

_____

What parts of your old life are you still associating with?

_____

_____

_____

What does the enemy keep bring back to you to keep you from moving forward?

_____

_____

_____

I want to give you some key things that will help you understand, you can only be free when you realize that you are already free. You are probably saying, what does that mean? When you realize you are free, it sets you free; then you can walk in your freedom. The entire story of Jesus is all about freedom and getting free. You must be free of yourself. First, say and believe, "I am not dealing with this anymore, I can be free. I accepted Jesus Christ at this point in my life; I am free, I am not tormented, I am not ridiculed." Receiving it brings manifestation.

Write a declaration based on this confession above.

_____

_____

_____

_____

_____

What does freedom look like to you?

_____

_____

_____

What access does freedom provide to the believer?

_____

_____

_____

When you focus on your freedom and apply Colossians 3:3 to your life, you will realize who you are in Christ. Once you do that, the next step is easy. We can battle this thing out, and remember the enemy has a right to do what he does because he has an assignment, but you have a higher power. Always recall that your appointment here is much higher than the enemy.

What is the believer's assignment?

_____

_____

_____

Identify and Teardown Idols:
Can you recognize what the idols are in your life? If so, what are they?

_____

_____

_____

When your identity becomes hidden or rooted in the revelation of who Jesus is and what He has already done, rather than looking at yourself and what you think is wrong with you, then you can live a better life.

How is a person's identity created?

_____
_____
_____

How is your identity defined in Christ?

_____
_____
_____
_____

God gives us a better life by His definition. Based on the identity Christ has given you, write a prayer outlining your authority and strength in your God-given identity.
_____
_____
_____
_____

Deliverance Focus #1: The Mindset

You must address the deliverance of your mind. You must guard your mind, the place the enemy affects you most. It begins when your mind wanders, and there is mind control. Mind control can be fear; it can be anxiety; it can be many things. In this mental process, when we talk about deliverance, the church leaves a crucial part out; we do not speak a lot about mental health.

Have you dealt with mind control in your life? If so, what have you experienced?

_____

_____

_____

How did it impact you?

_____

_____

_____

What does the bible say about the mind?

_____

_____

_____

What does the bible say we should do regarding the thoughts presented to our mind?

_____

_____

_____

Deliverance Focus #2: Know Who You Are

You are a new creature in Christ. Do not fall for the hype that Christians can be possessed. Christians cannot be possessed but can be oppressed; they can be depressed. You cannot be possessed if you are in Christ because He is living in you. He is the one that has you. We are going to get that part firm in your identity, because once you know your identity; it strips off insecurity. Identity strips off the complete picture of lack. It makes your mind open to thinking, this is who I am. That is the starting part of knowing who you are.

Who are you in Christ?

_____

_____

_____

What does the Word of God say regarding the throne room?

_____

_____

_____

How important is it to remove old mindsets?

_____

_____

_____

When you get free, you shall walk into those territories and pull things down and start doing the work that God has called you to do.

Complete the Deliverance Exercise on page 19 in the Deliverance For Real Book and write down what you learned.

_____

_____

_____

What clarity does freedom afford you so that you can help your fellow believers be free?

_____

_____

_____

Make these Daily Affirmations, begin to say them, and declare them! Write any additional affirmations that God has given you regarding freedom.

- I am not going through this anymore.
- I am not going to bed another night, upset.
- I am not going to bed another night being pulled and torn.
- I know who I am in Christ.
- I plead the blood of Jesus over my life.
- I am getting ready to rest.
- I am getting prepared to rise to a new place.
- I am getting ready to go into this place like never before.
- I close this gate in my mind because I understand my mind is at work, and I need to shut it down.
- I shut all these thoughts down.
- I am free of this control because I know it points me to fear, and fear leads us to anxiety.

_____

_____

How did you feel once you confessed the above statements?

_____

_____

_____

You must continually set a watch over your mind and ask yourself questions like:
- Is this genuine anxiety that I am feeling?
- Am I anxious because of everything that is going on in the world, or is this something I am battling?
- Am I trying to prove myself to somebody?

How important is it for you to shut down, rest, and regroup?

_____

_____

_____

What are some symptoms or signs that would let you know your mind is under attack?

_____

_____

_____

First Step: Identify the lies that the enemy has been bombarding your mind and write them down.

_____

_____

_____

Second Step: Identify that one thing that stays on your mind and write it below.

_____

_____

_____

Third Step: Apply the Word of God and start applying those scriptures you've heard over and over. Write down some of the scriptures that have impacted your life. Do they ring differently with this new information?

_____

_____

_____

Fourth Step: Affirm 2 Corinthians 10:4 (NLT), *We use God's mighty weapons, not worldly weapons, to knock down the strongholds of human reasoning and to destroy false arguments.* What does this scripture speak to you?

_____

_____

_____

Fifth Step: Understand and always recall, God is the one that is going to come in and cast down vain imaginations and everything that exalted itself against the knowledge of Him and bring into captivity every thought to the obedience of Christ. What assurance does this bring to mind?

_____

_____

_____

Sixth Step: Stop focusing on the enemy's opinions and bring into obedience to what God has said. During this lesson, what has God been speaking to your heart about you?

_____

_____

_____

Prayer of Activation:

Lord, set me free and heal me. I will walk in my deliverance. I am no longer just going to push my way through. Lord, I am whom You said I am. I am your child, and I am solid in that. This is not the life you intended for me. The gateway of my mind has been closed to thoughts that are not of you. Amen.

Key Takeaways:

_____

_____

_____

_____

_____

_____

_____

_____

Phase Two:
Demons and Demonic Legal Rights

Deliverance Focus #1: How Demons and Demonic Legal Rights Enter

These are very basic things in deliverance so that you will no longer push yourself back, whether you do deliverance or whether you need deliverance. Remember, deliverance is not always having a demon, deliverance is being free.

Entrance by Invitation

One way that the enemy will enter your life is through invitation, and sometimes that invitation is unknown to you. The enemy comes in our life, most of the time as a stronghold that has been erected, but sometimes it's simply by invitation. This means that we invite him into our life. When we seek knowledge of things and it's not through God, we give the enemy an invitation to come into our lives, and that sets up a stronghold. Normally, it'll happen when you would rebel against God, or even the authorities that are over you.

Read 1 Samuel 15:23, write the scripture out, and point out key points that invite the enemy into a life. Please keep in mind that rebellion is an attitude that brings on witchcraft.

_____

_____

_____

Define Witchcraft:

_____

_____

_____

Define Rebellion:

_____
_____
_____

Define Stubbornness:

_____
_____
_____

Based on the scripture and the definitions above has your idea of those words changed? If so how?

_____
_____
_____

Temptation

If you dangle a carrot in front of a donkey, or a rabbit, they grab it. The enemy uses this same tactic. Temptation often comes through the lust of the flesh or the lust of the eye according to James 1:14 KJV, *"But every man is tempted, when he is drawn away of his lust, and enticed."* Satan tempts every man when he's drawn away from his walk.

What has the enemy dangled in front of you?

_____
_____
_____

Intrusion of the Mind

Your thoughts can be a portal for an invitation. You can have condemning thoughts about yourself. Satan often intruded on Saul's thoughts.

Read I Samuel 18:10, write the scripture out, identify how the evil spirit impacted Saul? _____

_____

_____

_____

You cannot be afraid of Satan, he will meddle in your dream life; however, you have the Word of God and should apply it to your life. Never second guess who you are, or you'll never be free.

Can you identify areas where the enemy tried to invade your thoughts, vision, and dreams?

_____

_____

_____

_____

How has this impacted your life?

_____

_____

_____

_____

An Empty Mind

The enemy can enter through an empty mind. The Word warns us about an empty mind.

Read and write Matthew 12:43-45 List the actions of the unclean spirit.

_____

_____

_____

_____

_____

How important is it to fill the house once you have evicted the unclean spirit from the house?

_____

_____

_____

Why is it dangerous to have an empty mind?

_____

_____

_____

You must fill your mind with the words and promises of God and stop rehashing situations from the past.

Infatuation and Obsession

The enemy can also lure us through the trap of infatuation. For example, you are studying something that you should not be, such as Parapsychology (the supernatural). If you stay before the Lord, He will teach you all you need to know concerning the kingdom of God. Unfortunately, infatuation can lead to obsession. Obsession is bondage in itself.

Define Infatuation:

_____

_____

_____

Define Obsession:

_____

_____

_____

Based on the definition and the statement above list the dangers of living your life through these two words.

_____

_____

_____

_____

_____

We must remember to pay attention to the Word of God like our life depends on it, because it does. We are the victorious ones!

Unforgiveness

We must forgive! It's just that simple. We're either going to cast off the cares and walk in the cares of the Lord, or we will face the roaring lion.

Read and write 1 Peter 5:7-8.

_____

_____

_____

_____

What will the roaring lion do?

_____

_____

_____

Read and write Matthew 6:14-15

_____

_____

_____

_____

What is the benefit of forgiving? What is the disadvantage of not forgiving?

_____

_____

_____

Unforgiveness opens many doors for Satan to come into our lives. Unforgiveness can keep you bound for generations.

Stubbornness
In the bible, Asa became sick and died because of stubbornness, 2 Chronicles 16:12-13 NLT. *Doing things your way, when you want, and how you want despite repeated warnings.*

Define stubborn:

_____

_____

_____

The bible refers to stubbornness as stiff-necked. Stiff-necked is a demon that holds you in a stubborn state.

Read 2 Chronicles 30:8 and write the scripture. _____

_____

_____

_____

Define stiff-necked:

_____

_____

_____

What are the benefits of yielding to the Lord based on the scripture above?

_____

_____

_____

Negative Thoughts

Satan can enter when you keep focusing on negative thoughts. People always look at their glass as half full, that's not the mind of Christ. Remember when the 10 spies searched out the Promised Land (Numbers 13) and they came back with this evil report. Because all they could see was negative. All they could see was the giants and how big they were. There was a great statue. They couldn't see anything else.

Read Numbers 13 and list what the 10 spies all saw and their various reports are given to their leader.

_____

_____

_____

_____

Based on the scripture referenced above, how important is your perception to your vision?

_____

_____

What was the result for those who had a negative report versus those who had a positive report?

_____

_____

We're supposed to focus on Philippians 4:8 KJV, *"Finally, brethren, whatsoever things are true, whatsoever things are honest, whatsoever things are just, whatsoever things are pure, whatsoever things are lovely, whatsoever things are of good report; if there be any virtue, and if there be any praise, think on these things."* This will kill the enemy. If you believe what you say.

Based on the scripture above, list what the writer tells you to think on?

_____

_____

Now that you have the items listed, what benefits do you see if you think about these things?

_____

_____

Anger

The enemy can enter also through the door of anger. The first door of anger that was open to sin was Cain and Abel. The Bible says Cain was wrought. Which means very angry. It opened up a door to sin. Remember when you get angry; take a step back really quick, because anger can overtake you and before you know it, destruction. We can get angry, but we are to sin not according to Ephesians 4:26.

Read and write Ephesians 4:26-27, what do the authors convey about anger in the scripture?

_____
_____
_____
_____

In the story of Cain and Abel, Genesis 4:1-16, how destructive was the spirit of anger?

_____
_____
_____

What destructive fruit did the spirit of anger produce in this family?

_____
_____
_____

Scriptures to consider: Proverbs 14:29, Proverbs 15;1, Proverbs 21:14, Proverbs 27:4, Proverbs 29:8.

Generational Curses

Satan can enter through a generational curse. Let's look at word curses. There are two sides to word curses. First, you can place a negative judgment over others and the second-word curse occurs when there is negative communication by words. Negative communication impacts in various ways, when there are expressions when there are actions, especially those in authority. People in authority must be careful what you speak over people because it normally will come to pass.

Make a list of generational blessings and curses.

What statements have been spoken over you by authority figures that have impacted you, negatively or positively?

_____

_____

_____

The process of deliverance comprises three parts:
1. Recognizing strongholds
2. Removing legal rights
3. Casting out the remainder of demons

If you attempt to cast out demons and don't know their legal rights or what the stronghold is, then the deliverance process is incomplete.

Identify a situation that you need to renounce, list what was stated over you.

_____

_____

_____

_____

_____

Now that you have this information, construct and write out a prayer based on the guidance above.

_____

_____

_____

Deliverance Focus #2: Demonic Legal Rights
Willing Sinning

When we sin, it gives the enemy a legal right to affect or bother us in any way. The deeper the sin, the bigger the door that is open to the devil. The bigger it adds unholy thoughts in the mind, it opens the door to the demon of lust. For example, lust can lead to pornography, fornication, or adultery, but with a compulsion to do it. Demons then can push us into more sin. The remedy to this is repentance. Verbally confess and repent of your sins, then you restrain the enemy from having any legal rights in your life, but you got to recognize it.

Define the term legal right:

_____

_____

_____

Define Repentance:

_____

_____

_____

Can you identify areas in your life that have been opened by willful sin? If so notate the damage that has been created by these opened areas.

_____

_____

_____

Soul Ties

There are a lot of teachings on soul ties. I am old school. I believe soul ties come about from intimate relationships or having an infatuation with various things. Most of the time though, it is taught, the sin of adultery or fornication can open up and give demons legal rights. The remedy with that again is repentance, renunciation on the breaking of that soul tie, as well. A soul tie can hold you back, especially when there are physical objects involved from that person. You need to get rid of objects of affection, such as gifts.

Identify and list soul ties within your life.

_____

_____

_____

Are there some items that you need to remove from your life? If so what are they?

_____

_____

_____

Demonic Vow

Define vow:

_____
_____
_____

Define covenant:

_____
_____
_____

Before you make a covenant or vow you are to check everything before you commit. **With this knowledge, what vows or covenant have you made that you did not examine everything, and what were the results?**

_____
_____
_____

Childhood Rejection

Another arm to a demonic legal right is rejection. When a child is rejected, the spirit of rejection enters in, and then you must deal with the orphan spirit. A rejected person will spend all of their lives trying to live up to some expectations of another. The spirit of rejection causes a person to build walls (spiritual and emotional).

Define rejection:

_____
_____
_____

Define orphan:

_____
_____
_____

Can you identify any walls that you have built up due to rejection?

_____
_____
_____

Then bitterness can come in and make a person unapproachable. The enemy will use your weak spots against you. You must learn your weak spots so he cannot push your buttons and cause you to operate from a space of defeat.

Take this time now and identify and list any weak spots you may have in your life.

_____
_____
_____
_____

Define loneliness:

_____

_____

_____

What are some byproducts of loneliness?

_____

_____

_____

How does the word of God help you to address loneliness?

_____

_____

_____

Prayer of Activation:

Lord, we renounce word curses, and we break word curses in Jesus' name! I ask that you give me wisdom with my words that I no longer open doors unknowingly. I decree I will no longer use word curses. And when a word curse comes from somebody else, I will stop it in the atmosphere. I will shut it up. Lord, today, that is broken over my life; it will not manifest another day. Amen.

Key Takeaways:

Phase Three:
BIBLICAL AUTHORITY

In deliverance ministry, you must be knowledgeable of the Word of God and the giftings that work and are significant in deliverance. The following are spiritual gifts we apply:
- Word of knowledge
- Discerning of spirits
- The working of miracles
- Faith
- Healing

Read Luke 4:18-19 and write the scripture. Jesus Christ makes a declaration, list each point he stated.

_____

_____

_____

This declaration is from the Ministry of Deliverance.

Many terms are used from time to time in the deliverance ministry like inner healing. This is where the inward man has suffered emotionally and desires liberation from such pain. Inner healing is a key step in the overall restoration process taking place in the lives of many individuals who are seeking deliverance. Many times, when a person endures abuse, rejection, wounds, or hurt, there is an emotional wound that requires healing. In some instances, you may need inner healing and not the casting out of a demon. A demon has an attraction to the spiritual womb and the weaknesses of an individual. However, if you can minister to the area requiring inner healing and work through it, the individual can be delivered. For instance, someone did something to you, and you needed inner healing from abuse or something of that sort. The demon attacks that weak area. He plays on the weakest part of us. There is nothing new. He employs the same old thing each time. He builds on it. Sometimes you mention, well, I went through a deliverance session, and I shouldn't have to deal with that anymore, but did we get to the root? Did we discover the inner hurt? If we do not discover the root, you are going to go through the deliverance process again and again.

What are some examples in the word of God of inner healing and casting out of demons? _____

_____

_____

_____

_____

_____

Keep in mind, demons will use wounds and weaknesses as leverage to hold a person in bondage. Their primary goal is to get the person to reopen doors so they can keep coming back and forth.

Deliverance Focus #1: Tearing Down Strongholds

A stronghold is an incorrect thinking pattern people develop, set up, and is fueled by lies and deceptions. A stronghold is like a fortress of demons. They thrive on things like lies, deception, and use them to hang around and torment people. To better understand this a little more, I recommend besides this study you seek other resource materials on strongholds.

What thinking patterns have you developed that need to be torn down?

_____

_____

_____

Deliverance Focus #2: Removing Legal Rights

Legal rights are things that give demons permission to enter and remain in our lives. It is important before casting out demons you identify and remove all legal rights. Failing to remove a legal right can hold up the deliverance process.

Define the word legal:

_____

_____

_____

Define the word rights:

_____

_____

_____

Deliverance Focus #3: Taking Biblical Authority

The next term most people are familiar with is casting out demons. Many say I'm ready to cast out a demon; I'm ready to run the demon out; I'm ready to get rid of the demon. Well, first, recognize the authority and knowledge of your authority in Jesus Christ over the power of the enemy, and your faith in the authority Jesus has given you. It's not the faith you have that you can do it, but you have to have the faith in the authority Jesus has given you to do it. Once you have that, speak to and cast out the demons. Give them simple commands such as I command you to come out; I command you to go in the name of Jesus.

You must recognize what you are speaking to. For example, if you are speaking to a spirit of fear, you would say, I command the spirit of fear to leave now in the name of Jesus. You may say well, you should not talk to demons. However, in Mark 5:9, Jesus questioned a demon by asking what is your name? This does not differ from when a physician attended to you. He has no reservations when he asks for your medical history. He knows he cannot diagnose you until he receives the answers to certain questions.

In deliverance, we administer a deliverance questionnaire. The answers received will determine the root or source of the problem. At which point, we will see what we are dealing with and we can point you in the right direction.

Are we pointing you into inner healing? If so in what areas?

_____
_____
_____

Are we breaking up some legal ground? If so in what areas?

_____
_____
_____

Are we tearing down strongholds? If so what are they?

_____
_____
_____

What has your life been like?

_____
_____
_____

What has happened over time?

_____
_____
_____

What is your family lineage?

_____

_____

_____

Some places have different cultural practices. For instance, some countries practice satanic rituals such as sacrificing when a child is born, if it's a girl, or if it's something else. So, it is helpful to have a general idea of what you're dealing with. **Define the word cultural:**

_____

_____

_____

What are some of the cultural practices you currently live under?

_____

_____

_____

How has it impacted your spiritual walk?

_____

_____

_____

Can you identify if it is demonic activity, a health problem, or is it a mental issue?

_____

_____

Understand God wants to take your wounds, your pains, your hurts, and your sorrows. He gave His Son for us. Believe He loves you, Isaiah 53:4 NKJV says, *"Surely, he has borne our griefs and carried our sorrows, yet we esteemed him stricken; smitten of God and afflicted."* He cares about all our sorrows. He's worked all this out for us on the cross. Now once you understand, you will speak and trust that God loves you and healing can occur.

What are the issues that God provided a remedy for on the cross?

_____

_____

_____

Jesus has paid the price for us. He loves us, and it's not because of anything we've done, but everything He's done. If we do not understand the love of the Father, we will deal with another spirit called the Orphan Spirit. This spirit makes you assume you must do something for someone to care about you.

What areas in your life have you performed rather than walked in the acceptance of the Father?

_____

_____

_____

When you have the love of God, you have it all and you do not have to do anything else. His will is for us to be free. He wants us to be free from abuse, trauma, hurt, and pain. These are the workings of the enemy. However, what did Jesus do? He came to destroy the works of the enemy and to restore us to the purpose in which he created us. Acts 10:38 NKJV says, *"How God anointed Jesus of Nazareth with the Holy Ghost and with power, who went about doing good and healing all that were oppressed of the devil for God was with Him."*

What does this scripture confirm about Jesus' desire toward our total wholeness?

_____

_____

_____

In ministering deliverance, forgiveness is a major component. We must forgive those who have hurt us. If not, like a deadly poison, unforgiveness will hinder or block the very healing power of the Lord. It separates us from God and opens doors for tormenting spirits. Have you ever heard people say, "I am having trouble sleeping"? The question is, what are you still holding on to? Learn how to let things go and in letting go, you will release feelings of bitterness. You are asking for total restoration for your spirit. It is only when we forgive others, the healing power of the Holy Spirit can flow into our lives. As a result, the healing process begins. However, in cases where a person seems to display difficulty receiving their complete healing, most of the time the root cause is unforgiveness. They ask, "Why didn't my healing last?" Not that God didn't release the healing. It was the unforgiveness in your heart you could not get past. It was the wrong someone had done against you, that kept you from receiving your healing. Once you can forgive those that wronged you, deliverance can happen and stop you from experiencing the same thing over and over again. It is unforgiveness that will keep you separated from the healing power of God. Therefore, you must release those feelings you hold against others. We must forgive so we can move forward.

Is unforgiveness still active in your life? If so, why are you still holding on to it?

_____

_____

_____

If not, what revelation did you receive that allowed you to let it go?

_____
_____
_____

The enemy has a job to do, and that is to torment us so we will lose our identity in Christ. He wants to keep us from doing what God has called us to do; that is to reach others and to fulfill the Great Commission.

Read and write Matthew 28:18-20 and outline the calling Jesus spoke over the disciples. _____

_____
_____
_____
_____
_____

Forgiving oneself is vital to one's deliverance. You cannot keep beating yourself up because of past mistakes and failures. Jesus has washed them all away.

Why do people keep going back and forth once they have been forgiven?

_____
_____
_____

When you keep reminiscing over your past, you are denying the work of the cross. Forgive yourself and be set free. The scripture says in John 8:36, _"if the son, therefore, shall make you free, ye shall be free indeed."_ So, stop beating yourself up about the past, God washed it away. It is over.

Complete the Deliverance Exercise starting on page 38 in the Deliverance For Real Book and write down what you learned.

_____

_____

_____

IMPORTANT NOTE

If you are not a believer in Christ, I do not recommend you confront any evil spirit until you become a believer. Because the demons realize you are not a believer and you do not possess the power to cast them out. Matter of fact, as an unbeliever, where would you send them and, in whose name would you use? You cannot use Jesus' name because you do not know Him. Remember, demonic spirits are powerful, but they are not all-powerful. Jesus has all power and without Him, you cannot disarm any evil spirit. Since you are reading this book, now you have the chance to accept Jesus as your personal Savior. It is not hard; let us go before him with this simple prayer.

"Lord Jesus, I realized I'm a sinner. I believe You died and shed your blood just for me. I believe You did it for the remission of my sins and to give me eternal life. So right now, I turn away from my sins and I ask You to come into my life; change me into a new person; and wash away all my sins. I receive You as my personal Lord and Savior. Amen."

If you prayed the prayer with me, believed in your heart, and confessed to Jesus as Lord, you accepted Jesus as your personal Savior. Your new walk with Him has started. Surround yourself with people that can help you walk through the process of deliverance.

The following are simple things you can now do:
- Come against unclean spirits influencing your mind, your will, and your emotion.
- Learn how to take authority over spirits in the mighty name of Jesus
- Command the spirits to depart from you.

In casting out spirits, you do not have to scream loud, because demons can hear you. God has given you this authority. However, if you need more assistance, I recommend you seek out a church that operates in deliverance or a strong deliverance minister. In deliverance, you must understand authority. We do not do any of this in our authority. It's all done in God's authority. In understanding His authority, we can understand ours. Mark 13:34 conveys the authority given to believers. We have the authority to heal the sick, to cleanse the lepers, to raise the dead, and to cast out demons.

Prayer of Activation:

Lord Jesus, I love You; I thank You for bearing all my burdens at the cross. I ask You to take the inner hurt. I ask You to take the painful memories. I ask that You take the emotional feelings. I ask that You take it away from me now. And I submit to You, Lord, and I accept your peace because once something is taken away, something must be replaced. I accept your peace in exchange for the things I am now giving up. I am releasing the pain of _____ (Enter your pain points here using this example: I am releasing the pain that rape at 10 years old. I release that pain of the abuse. I release that man or woman who left me. I am releasing the fact they did not give me that job.) God, I am releasing all this pain, because You took care of everything for me. I accept your peace. So now, I am asking You to take care of this and I am going to back out your way and let You come in. I receive Your love, no greater love. Because there is no substitution for your love. In Jesus' name, Amen!

Key Takeaways:

_____

_____

_____

_____

_____

_____

_____

Phase Four:
INNER HEALING

1 John 14:12 and Matthew 10:1 are biblical authority scriptures. If you're having issues and you feel like the enemy is trying to take over your home or is trying to take you over, go back to the scriptures and read and live them out.

Write down vital points you identified in the above scriptures and make them into daily affirmations.

_____

_____

_____

_____

Deliverance Focus #1: Casting Out Legal Rights
What does the term legal rights mean?

_____

_____

_____

What are the key parts in the process of deliverance?

_____

_____

_____

_____

What are some of the common legal rights?

_____

_____

_____

One of the key things that give demons a legal right is unforgiveness and there are sexual sins or (ancestral sins), childhood rejection, points of weakness, and spoken self-curses. You know we can speak over our self and curse ourselves, sometimes a cursed object, refer to Old Testament scripture, Leviticus 18:27.

Read and write Leviticus 18:26-28 and list key points that brought about a curse for the people. _____

_____

_____

_____

_____

How did the curse impact all involved?

_____

_____

_____

_____

How dangerous is false teaching/doctrine?

How can it impact your spiritual walk with God?

Deliverance Focus #2: Experiencing Inner Healing

Inner healing is a vital step in overall restoration. You can say you're okay, you can say you are doing fine with this, but this inner healing piece is the first vital step in the overall restoration process. See, you cannot be free until you want to be free.

Read and write out the key scripture for inner healing, Ephesians 4:15.

What is real inner healing?

How important is belief in the deliverance process?

_____

_____

_____

The aim of inner healing is not to patch you up, but it is for you to have a transformation that can move you from that rape, from that molestation, and transform you. So, we can say that inner healing is the healing of memories and you need prayer, and you need counseling in these things.

Can you outline any areas in your life where you need inner healing?

_____

_____

_____

Let us pray a prayer as we begin to talk about inner healing, because inner healing as you talk about it, hits places on the inside of you. So, there will not be any recoiling and striking back, you are going to have a peaceful night's sleep.

Prayer of Activation:

Father, on this day we thank You and we reverence You for your knowledge You have given us from on high. We open ourselves up to allow the healing process to begin. We say God let the bitter root be dug out for forgiveness, for cleansing; that it all begins now. We acknowledge that none of this could happen without the Holy Spirit, for direction. So, we pray for divine revelation for our inner healing. We thank You for the beginning of our fresh eyes. We thank You for the change in our hearts. We put on the whole armor of God so it can protect us and our choice is you, and we will learn how to live as You desire. Amen.

The healing process begins first with a simple prayer. To achieve healing, we must get to the root. Hebrews 12:15 gives us guidance as a believer.

Read and write Hebrews 12:15. Define the instructions in the scripture.

What is a bitter root?

How can it affect you as a believer?

You cannot pull up a bitter root, you must dig it up. How important is it to dig it up?

Define wounds:

_____

_____

_____

Identify and write down the prior wounds that could potentially be hindrances to your deliverance.

_____

_____

_____

Inner healing begins through communication with God, you must talk about that thing. Prayer is communication where you talk about your issues with Jesus.

Write a prayer outlining the issues you need to share with the Father?

_____

_____

_____

_____

_____

Remember, the scriptures are our promise, and the Lord speaks through them. When reading the scriptures, I would advise you to ask the Lord to give a mental picture, because to every one of you what the scripture says is a revelation to you. My revelation may not be your revelation; however, the revelation you receive will be what you need to pull you out of it. So that is the key thing.

Take this time now and record the revelation the scripture has presented thus far in this study.

_____

_____

_____

_____

_____

The healing begins first within your heart where truth is revealed. Healing also begins with this big word, forgiveness.

Define forgiveness:

_____

_____

_____

You can only forgive by the grace of God. He forgave so we might forgive as well. This takes work on your behalf.

Write some scriptures that reinforce forgiveness in your life.

_____

_____

_____

_____

What is an unbelieving heart?

_____

_____

_____

What is the answer to the unbelieving heart?

_____

_____

_____

Inner healing does not erase the memory, you are going to have the memory. It does not change your personal history; however, it enables you to cherish even the worst moments in your life. Remember, even the very worst moment in your life is a stepping-stone, it is a building place for you.

How can the memory be used as a stepping stone?

_____

_____

_____

How can you use the memory to minister to someone else?

_____

_____

_____

The key to your inner healing piece for staying free is an acknowledgment of what your fear is because a lot of times, we do not stay free simply because we have not acknowledged what that fear was.

Take this time now and write out the areas in your life that fear has resided. Allow this exercise to begin to address the areas of your heart that you have failed to investigate.

_____

_____

_____

_____

_____

Deliverance Exercise:

Some Principles to Stay Free
- Celebrate you are free.
- Keep non-accusing people around you, those who are not going to always bring up your failures.

What is the benefit of the two statements above?

_____

_____

_____

Some Principles for Freedom in Christ
- First Principle: Confessing the general area in which you have received freedom.

Read and write out Romans 10:9-10. Write out your confession of deliverance based on this scripture.

_____

_____

_____

_____

_____

_____

- Second principle: Meet each new day trusting in God's power to help you make the right choices. Do not let your feelings deceive you.

How will you meet each day trusting in God's power?

_____

_____

_____

- Third Principle: Expect a continuous increase in freedom.

How will you move forward by faith?

_____

_____

_____

- Fourth Principle: Rely upon the Holy Spirit to control your life.

Write the prayer asking the Lord I need you to help me control my life, my emotions, my desires, my imaginations, all by and with your will.

_____

_____

_____

_____

_____

- Fifth Principle: Extend forgiveness to those who have hurt you and always realizing who you are in Christ. a. Stop feeding on lies.

Utilizing the principles above, write out your daily action plan.

_____

_____

_____

Read and write 2 Corinthians 10:5. List the steps outlined for dealing with your thought life.

_____

_____

_____

_____

Do we have the ability to take every thought captive?

_____

_____

_____

Pray a simple prayer of deliverance.
I come against every unclean spirit that has influenced my mind, my will, and my emotions, and I take authority over these spirits, in the name of Jesus.

Take Authority.
I take authority over these spirits in the name of Jesus, I command any such spirit; I command it to come out and depart from me, every part of me, in the name of Jesus

Make these declarations:
- I am a child of God!
- I am a King's Kid!

Key Points to Address:
- Be sure of who you are
- Be sure of what you are doing
- Be sure of how you are moving forward

Inner healing and deliverance, there are different realms. You can operate in the flesh realm, in the demonic realm, in the soulish realm, or the natural realm. However, you should operate in the realm of the Holy Spirit or the supernatural realm and allow God to take charge of everything.

What realm have you been living your life from?

_____

_____

_____

Identify and write down your emotional wounds.

Key Takeaways:

Phase Five: REJECTION

Rejection and the fear of rejection will warp, distort, or twist the perception of God.

Define rejection:

_____

_____

_____

When did the fear of rejection first enter the world? Please list the event and the bible verse.

_____

_____

_____

How did Adam and Eve respond due to fear of rejection?

_____

_____

_____

Prayer of Activation:

Father, I repent of all deception. I repent of all lying; I repent of suspicion; I repent of mistrust. I repent of control, and I repent of manipulation. Lord, I repent of trying to please people and have their approval instead of seeking You. I renounce the spirit of the fear of rejection. I break off soul ties and generational curses. And I break down the wall of the fear of rejection in Jesus' name; I declare the wall is broken, and I am set free. Amen!

Deliverance Focus #1: Self-Rejection
What is self-rejection?

_____

_____

_____

Self-rejection produces the following and they must be addressed.
- Low self-esteem
- Feelings of worthlessness
- Hopelessness
- Depression
- If not addressed (feelings of suicide)

Prayer of Repentance:

Father, I repent for rejecting myself; I repent from hating your creation, and I repent for resisting your plan for my life. I repent of trying to be someone that I was never meant to be. I repent for always looking for approval and the acceptance of others. Spirit of self-rejection, I renounce you, and I break your power and your authority over me. I break every curse. I break every vow that gave you a legal right to my life. Lord, I choose to accept the love of Jesus Christ for myself, for I know who I am in Christ Jesus. I accept God's love; I accept God's ways and His will for my life. I break the stronghold of rejection. I am not going after anyone else until I go after myself first. I rid myself of self-rejection now, in Jesus' name. Holy Spirit, I thank You for accepting me and filling me with your presence. I now choose to accept myself as one that God has accepted. Amen.

Deliverance Focus #2: Rejection of Others

This Phase deals with rejection (the fear of rejection), and self-rejection and they have built a fortress. Picture this, we had a load-bearing wall, and then we had all these other walls around. Walls built against God. Walls built against us, and walls constructed against others. Now, we are tearing down the walls. The last barrier is to tear down the rejection of others. The rejection of others causes you to transfer blame to others for your problems

Be aware of negative statements we make:
- If only they were more loving
- If they were more caring

- If they were more supportive
- If they had only kept their promises, things would have been different.

How could we take these negative statements and make them positive confessions? _____

_____

_____

_____

Prayer for Rejecting Others:

Father, I repent for rejecting others. I repent for being resentful. I repent for being bitter. I repent from being unforgiving toward others. I repent for rejecting people because of the hurt I experienced from other people. I renounce the spirit of rejection of others, and I break that power of rejection of others. I recognize it, and I break that power over me. I break the power of all words and all negative words. I break the power of agreement; I break the power of soul ties. I break the power of generational curses. I refuse this influence over my life. Today, I have dismantled the rejection of others. And I declare that there is no more recoiling and striking back to keep me in bondage. Christ has already defeated all of this at the cross and because of that authority and the power that Jesus has given me, I command you to loose me from your hold and I choose to allow the Holy Spirit to fill me.

Many people, who have faced rejection, experienced abuse as children, or may have unresolved emotional wounds. Rejection causes emotional or spiritual wounds first, and if we do not address it, you will grow up with a wounded or vested spirit. Unforgiveness, Blaming God, Envy and Jealousy are areas of rejection that will have to be addressed.

When did rejection enter your life?

_____

_____

_____

Based on the list above, can you now give a name to that area of rejection? If so, what is it?

_____

_____

Define Spiritual Wound:

_____

_____

Complete the Deliverance Exercise on page 62. Write down your emotions as you put the items in the bag.

_____

_____

_____

_____

Define Fabricated Personality:

_____

_____

Define Self-Pity:

_____

_____

_____

Define Insecurity:

_____

_____

_____

Define Strong-willed Personality:

_____

_____

_____

Define Rejected Fixers:

_____

_____

_____

Rejection is a form of an antichrist. Antichrist means against Christ. Rejection in this form says that love cannot be given, which opposes God's very nature. God is love according to 1 John 4:8.

Read and write 1 John 4:8 and list the key points about love.

_____

_____

_____

Define misplaced identity:

_____

_____

_____

How do you get rid of it?

_____

_____

_____

What does the Word of God say concerning who you are based on 1 Peter 2:9?

_____

_____

_____

    Authority figures can also deeply cause rejection wounds. If you are dealing with rejection and that authority figure does not know, and they could say something to you that devastates you. This is why discernment is key.

Define discernment:

_____
_____
_____

Read the following scriptures Hebrews 13:5, Romans 8:7, and Ephesians 2:6. In these scriptures, who does the Lord say we are and what responsibility has He taken in our lives?

_____
_____
_____

Another rejection that must be exposed is emotional abuse or intentional rejection. This type of rejection can be deep and very painful. Inner healing can combat emotional abuse or intentional rejection.

Steps to Deliverance in Inner Healing:
- Inner Healing
- Have power over your thoughts
- Know how God sees you
- Keep a forgiving heart

How is your heart toward the person who rejected you?

_____
_____
_____
_____

Read and write 2 Corinthians 2:11. What does the scripture say about the devices of Satan?

_____

_____

_____

_____

_____

Define repentance:

_____

_____

_____

Prayer of Activation:

Father, I thank You. I thank You for repentance. I repent for rejecting You, myself, and others. I repent of preconceived ideas. God, I thank You for your word that tells me of my true identity. I thank You that I am free. God, I pray that no weapon formed against me shall prosper. I know that the enemy comes to steal, kill and destroy, but You came that I may have life and life more abundantly. God, I praise You and I exalt You. I am excited because You have set a standard for my life and I choose to walk by that standard. God, I believe that your word is true; I thank You for loving me and for keeping me going in this season. Father, I thank You that I am moving into a greater season. Amen!

Key Takeaways:

_____

_____

_____

Phase Six:
SPIRITUAL CONTAMINATION AND INTRUSION

During this phase, please keep in mind Acts 15:20, *"We write to them to abstain from things polluted by idols from sexual immorality, from things strangled, and from blood."* Sin gives the enemy a legal foothold in our lives. There are 3 different areas where footholds can enter and grant the enemy access. Sin is the primary way he gains access to our lives as well as through spiritual contamination and ancestral sins.

Deliverance Focus #1: Spiritual Contamination

Spiritual contamination in our lives hinders the Spirit's flow, and it creates an opening for demons to operate. It occurs when unclean things or objects pollute our lives.

Review your home and identify objects you have received that could present a foothold for the enemy in your life. List them below.

_____
_____
_____
_____

Define accursed:

_____
_____
_____

The most prominent form of spiritual contamination is a statute. The statues that are erected throughout the land represent something. Many of them we see represent oppression, depression, and it is an object of worship. It can even be something that people with various faiths worship and/or what their mind has deemed it to be. I would consider this an idol.

Identify things within the culture that could be accursed and represent spiritual contamination?

_____

_____

_____

Define idol:

_____

_____

_____

Read Ezekiel 8:1-18 and list the various idols the Lord told Ezekiel to witness and His feeling toward them.

_____

_____

_____

_____

_____

Read and write Deuteronomy 27:15. What does God say about carven or molded images?

_____

_____

_____

_____

_____

Read Joshua 7:6-13 regarding the accursed thing. What happened to the children of Israel?

_____

_____

_____

Read and write 2 Corinthians 6:17 and 2 Corinthians 7:1. What are the instructions given in these scriptures to help remove spiritual contamination?

_____

_____

_____

_____

Deliverance Exercise:
Matters Concerning Your Home

Have you dedicated your home to the Lord?
- o Yes
- o No

Have you asked Him to use it for His purpose?
- o Yes
- o No

Have you asked God to allow His presence to remain in your home?
- o Yes
- o No

If not, take this moment right now and ask the Father to abide in your home and let his purpose be fulfilled.

Now, take a spiritual inventory of your home. Ask for discernment as you go through your house, room by room, and let the Holy Spirit show you objects that should not be in your home. This may include stuff you like and even some things gifted to you. Do a complete walk-through to make sure nothing is representing a false god, there's no pagan worship associated with it, and that there's nothing promoting something that's not of God.

Write down the items you collected for removal.

_____

_____

_____

_____

_____

_____

If you discover an artifact, statue, or anything offensive in your home, ask the Lord for forgiveness on your behalf. Even though you were not aware, repent of and renounce any type of participation you may have.

Go out and walk on your land, walk around your house, plead the blood of Jesus over your property. Pray over your property and decree and declare that no demonic forces are coming through your door. The reason being, you never know the activity or who may have walked up and down your property during the day or night.

We must make sure we repent of every known and unknown covenant, any covenants that could have brought curses, pledges, and uproot every evil root in Jesus' name. Ask the Lord to cancel every written covenant agreement, any record of sin against it, and let it be nailed on the cross. We are ready for this to be over in the name of Jesus.

Write your prayer to renounce spiritual contamination in your home and land.

_____

_____

_____

_____

_____

_____

_____

Prayer of Activation:

First, we repent of every known and unknown covenant. Father, I ask in your precious name that I am purged with your blood, let this be for my spirit, mind, body, and soul. I am no longer trapped by anger, lust, or bitterness. No more self-sabotage! I cancel the works of idol worship in my life. No more false altars being built, no more secret sins. I surrender all to the Father. I replace every curse with a blessing. I believe that there is no more pollution. In Jesus' name, Amen!

Deliverance Focus # 2: Intrusion

Define Intrusion:

_____
_____
_____

5 Open Doors That Invites Intrusion:
1. Disobedience:
What am I doing that is causing me to be in bondage?

_____
_____
_____

What am I doing unwillingly and unknowingly?

_____
_____
_____

2. Unforgiveness:
What is your definition of forgiveness?

_____
_____
_____

Read and write Matthew 6:12. Where does forgiveness come from?

_____
_____
_____

3. Emotional Trauma
Define Emotional Trauma:

_____
_____
_____

Write down the emotional traumas that have occurred in your life.

_____
_____
_____

How did you deal with those traumas and do you feel as though you have gained resolution?

_____
_____
_____
_____

4. Inner Vows and Judgements

Define inner vow:

_____

_____

Have you ever made an inner vow or judgment? If so what was the vow?

_____

_____

5. Curses
What are some types of curses?

_____

_____

5 Primary Strategies that Can Cause Intrusion:
1. Lies and Deception

Define lie:

_____

_____

Define Deception:

2. Accusation and Condemnation
Define Accusation:

Define Condemnation:

3. Doubt, Unbelief, and Fear
Define Doubt:

Define Unbelief:

Define Fear:

_____

_____

_____

In what areas has the enemy tried to speak doubt, unbelief, and fear in your life?

_____

_____

_____

4. The Battle of the Mind
Read and write 2 Corinthians 10:3-4. How does the believer wage war?

_____

_____

_____

_____

What are the weapons you use to wage war? What type of power do our weapons possess?

_____

_____

_____

5. Attacking the Word of God

Read the scripture Matthew 4;1—11. How does Jesus' command of the word defeat the enemy?

_____

_____

_____

How important is belief in the word of God?

_____

_____

_____

Deliverance Exercise
When you get blindsided what are a few things to keep in mind?

_____

_____

_____

_____

Read and write James 4:7. What is the strategy given to the believer in this scripture?

_____

_____

_____

What does the scripture say the outcome will be if you use this strategy?

Prayer of Activation:

I ask the Father to illuminate my mind and heart for clarity. Let angels protect my home, my family, and my mind. I claim the hedge of protection. Every open door of intrusion, I close it now. All intruders and illegal squatters must leave. No more illegal intrusion to this temple. Lord Jesus, cover my mind and heart. In Jesus' name, Amen!

Key Takeaways:

Phase Seven:
BINDING AND LOOSING

Let me explain to you about forbidding authority and allowing authority, a principle of binding and loosing. Loose means you release something. The enemy did the binding; this is a controversial statement of binding and loosening. Can you bind up the devil? No, you cannot, and I think we need to study this so that we can have clarity of a thing.

Define Bind:

_____

_____

_____

Define Loose:

_____

_____

_____

Read and write Matthew 16;19. What is your understanding of the scripture?

_____

_____

_____

_____

_____

Define Keys:

What is the difference between Satan and evils spirits?

Read and write Luke 10:17. Who are the demons subject to?

What authority did He give us?

What three things should you keep in mind when dealing with fear?

Define the two sources of fear:

_____

_____

_____

Spirit of Jezebel

It is a spirit that comes to rob you of your destiny, the destined place God designed for you. It comes with all kinds of other attachments, with familiar spirits.

Define Familiar Spirits:

_____

_____

_____

Deliverance Exercise
How to Defeat Demons
<u>The Holy Spirit</u>
Jesus operated under the direction and the power of the Holy Spirit.

Do you have the Holy Spirit?
- No. You do not have the Holy Spirit, ask the Lord to give you the Holy Spirit.
- Yes. You have the Holy Spirit, ask the Lord to fill you again.

Read and write Matthew 12:28 NLT. What comes to us through the baptism in the Holy Spirit?

_____

_____

_____

The Scripture
Jesus uses the scriptures; therefore, we are to quote scriptures as Jesus did.

Read Luke 4. What did Jesus use against temptation and what should we turn to for our calmness and solutions?

_____

_____

Read and write Isaiah 54:17. What in this passage of scripture stands out to you?

_____

_____

_____

_____

The Spirit of Fear
Define Fear:

_____

_____

_____

Read and write 2 Timothy 1:7. What remedy did God give for the spirit of fear?

_____

_____

_____

_____

The Blood of the Lamb

What does the word of God say about the Blood of the Lamb? Write 5 scriptures that speak of the Blood of the Lamb.

_____
_____
_____

The Word of Our Testimony

Read and write Revelation 12:11. Take this opportunity and write your testimony.

_____
_____
_____
_____
_____
_____
_____
_____
_____

Rejoice and celebrate the victory of what the Lord has brought you through!

Taking All Our Thoughts Captive
Read and write 2 Corinthians 10:3-5.

_____

_____

_____

_____

Define Warfare:

_____

Define Carnal:

_____

Define Stronghold:

_____

_____

With the scripture and definitions above, what does the scripture say regarding warfare and the believer's stance?

_____

_____

_____

_____

The Authority Given to Us in Christ

Read and write Luke 10:19 NLT. Under what authority are you able to cast them out?

_____

_____

_____

Define cast out:

_____

_____

_____

We Defeat Demons:

1. By Spiritual Warfare:
Read Write the following scripture Ephesians 6:10-12 NLT.

_____

_____

_____

Define strategies:

_____

_____

_____

Who does the word state you are fighting? List them below.

_____

_____

Is the battle spiritual or physical? Based on your answer what is the outcome if you fight spiritually or physically?

_____

_____

<u>Through intercessory prayer</u>
Define intercession:

_____

_____

Based on this definition of intercession how has this changed your point of view about intercessory prayer?

_____

_____

<u>By thanksgiving, praise, and worship.</u>
How important are thanksgiving, praise, and worship to a believer's life?

_____

_____

List scriptures that speak of thanksgiving, praise, and worship.

_____

_____

How do these scriptures speak to your life as a believer?

_____

_____

Deliverance Focus #1 - Mislabeling

In churches, we have mislabeled the demonic. We must realize that we're dealing with three areas: (1) medical, (2) mental, or (3) demonic. We need to investigate our bloodlines to see what is going on.

Can you list any issues that have run through your bloodline?

_____

_____

_____

What area had you previously assigned the issue to before this revelation and why?

_____

_____

_____

Deliverance Focus #2 – Baptism in the Holy Spirit

If you are not baptized in the Holy Ghost, you need to get baptized in the Holy Ghost.

What is one of your weapons?

_____

Take this time and write your experience with God.

_____

_____

_____

What are some qualities of a servant's heart/attitude?

_____

_____

_____

What are the benefits of having a servant's heart?

_____

_____

_____

What was the ministry of Jesus?

We must hate what Jesus hates and love what He loves.
List some things found in scripture that outline these two criteria.

How important is it for you to have a listening ear and how does the listening ear play a part in deliverance?

What items do you need in a deliverance session?

What role does discernment play in deliverance?

What do you believe will hold you back in deliverance ministry?

_____

_____

_____

Deliverance Focus #3 – Do's and the Don'ts
1. Don't go around telling people you know how they feel.
2. Understand that demons come out in three different ways
   - Right Away
   - Over some time
   - Many days
3. Don't feel you need an answer for everything
4. Don't wear yourself out
5. Don't go into a session weak feeling
6. Don't become a person's permanent crutch
7. Teach people how to do self-deliverance
8. Don't step in and take the place of the Holy Spirit
9. Do give them some instructions
10. Do not advise anything.
11. Do not go into a session telling people what to do.
12. Don't advise people to throw away their medicine
13. You must be confidential
14. Do not be alone with anyone in private. Two by two
15. False concept is Christians can't have demons. Yes, Christians can have demons.

Based on the list above is there anything in this list that is surprising to you? If so, what is it and why?

_____

_____

_____

_____

Prayer of Activation:

Father, I thank You for the ones who are reading this book. God, I pray something was stated that affected them in a way that they will move forth in the things of You. And Father, we say no weapon formed against them shall prosper; every tongue that is rising to condemn them, God, we say that they have just opened their mouths and open their mind to a new place in You. So, we thank You God that we are not giving the enemy any credit that we are glorifying and magnifying You. We are praising You, God, for this season at this time in our life. God, we know we're coming through everything all right and we are powerful because You said so. Amen!

Key Takeaways:

_____

_____

_____

_____

_____

_____

_____

_____

_____

Phase Eight:
TRAUMA PHASE

Deliverance Focus Five KEY Truths That the Scriptures Teach About Trauma and Suffering

1. God is present, and He is in control.
2. God is good all the time, and He cares for us.
3. Consider it pure joy when we go through tough times.
4. Jesus understands what it is to suffer.
5. Our identity is not defined by a traumatic event or suffering, but our identity is grounded in Christ.

What can trauma bring?

_____

_____

_____

Read and write out the following scriptures and list how they can be used to minister healing and deliverance:

Isaiah 61:1: _____

_____

_____

_____

Isaiah 51:12: _____

_____

_____

_____

2 Corinthians 1:3: _____
_____
_____
_____

James 5:16: _____
_____
_____
_____

Zechariah 2:8: _____
_____
_____
_____

Prayer of Activation:

This is a passion ministry; a passion of loving people and you have to love them the way God loves them. Your heart must beat like God's heart beats; you must have compassion. This is not a ministry where you get to pick and choose.

Pray this prayer for yourself:
There will be no manifestation we take full authority over that in the name of Jesus. This prayer is being released to heal those that are hurting, those that are reading this for someone else so that they can also share.

Lord Jesus, I asked You to bring peace to name here and establish your dominion and your peace; manifest yourself in such a way name here will know You are here and allow him/her to feel the depths of your love. I asked You, Lord because this is scripture. I asked You to rebuke any forces of darkness that seek to harm him/her in any way or have tried to keep him/her locked in this prison of trauma. You have not given us a spirit of fear, but of love, power, and soundness of mind, and that it is what I claim for everyone repeating this prayer. As we pray, Lord, I asked that You would be like a sponge and You would draw all the pain, the trauma, the shock, the fear, the terror, the shame that is bringing it all down to the foot of the cross. You suffered and died for us all and we thank You for all that You have accomplished in us thus far. So, pour your love and your grace by the power of the Holy Spirit and remove the traumatic memory that has been stored in the cells of their body and restore those cells to perfect order. Bring the body back into a state of homeostasis that's a stabling place. Lord, I bless the very moment of conception when they came into the world. I bless every moment that was in their mother's womb, Holy Spirit, I ask You to hover over the original DNA and restore all the frequencies, all the tones, everything and remove anything that is not like You.

Heavenly Father, I asked You to remove the traumatic experiences in the womb, absorbed from the womb trauma that's been passed down through generation to generation. I asked You for the very DNA to be healed, and that they would understand the DNA of Jesus Christ. Remove the shock remove the trauma, remove the fear, remove the terror, and remove the shame that flows from generation to generation. Forgive them God in their generation and let everything stop now at the cross. Forgive them, Lord Jesus, forgive the past generations, for those that traumatized, manipulated, dominated, and controlled through fear and torment. Release your precious blood and heal all the unresolved grief and pain.

Lord, I bless their rebirth now, and I call them forth into the newness of life. I say that they're welcome on this earth. They will no longer say I want out of here. No, there is a place established for them here. There's a purpose for them here and there's a plan to give them a future and a hope and to prosper in every way. Heavenly Father, I pray You to bring healing. Please remove the shock and the trauma and the fear and the terror that's in them that was experienced during this birthing process. Let them now embrace life like never before, I asked You to come into that conscious and the subconscious memory right now. Remove the shock, trauma, and pain that caused so much injury. I ask You, Lord God, to work on the mind and the brain. God, go into each part of the frontal lobe. Remove the shock, remove the pain, remove the fear and remove this emotion. I ask You to bring healing to the fear in the center of their brain. Turn off the anxiety that's been present for so long. Replace the fear. God give them godly discernment. Let them know whether there is a true danger. God don't let them walk thinking suspiciously of everyone. Give the wisdom. Let them know when it's a true danger and how to deal with it. Bring peace and rest to the part of their heart that's needed. The part of their heart that's always standing guard, the part of their heart that's always on alert. Remove that low-level anxiety, heal the immune system, remove all the toxins that remain from the chemicals and the hormones that over poured into their body for years. Remove the trauma from the eyes and the ears, wash away the images that were seared on their soul. Wash it away with the blood of Jesus and remove the trauma from the words that have been spoken, remove it from disharmony, disease, disorder, take it and bring ease. Take and bring the order that the words and all these images have caused them. Sing your love song over them, Lord, bring everything into an agreement with your word and with your original design.

Father, we prophesy order. We prophesy healing. We prophesy in their mind. We prophesy in their body, and we prophesy in their spirit. Remove any trauma or shame that's associated with a scent. Remove any trauma from the skin. Lord, I pray You to shake up their very core and their very foundation. I ask that You heal every crack in them with your love. Father, I ask You to restore trust and grace, that they believe in You and that they receive Your promises and that they trust You so that they can move and walk into that place. I asked for restoration. I asked for strength. I ask You, Lord, to remove blockages that have caused the limbs to be weak that has caused the muscles to be weak. God, I asked You to bring healing power, where they are crushed, where they are broken. I asked You to restore health. I asked You to restore vitality. I ask that You restore vigor. I asked You, God, that You make their connective tissues strong. I ask that You remove this shock, this trauma, this fear, this terror from all the organs of their body.

Oh, God, I ask that You remove all unhealthy soul ties that have been created through trauma. I break every assignment now in the name of Jesus of trauma against everyone reading these words and those that they will go and pray for others. I bind, and I send away every spirit guard that's assigned to them. We receive and we are appreciating the love, power, and soundness of mind that has been promised and given to us. And Lord, we bring death to old ways of responding and reacting to shock, fear, and trauma. We dismantle this ungodly structure of defense, and we establish a new way of thinking, a new neurological connection to having a joy center, rebuild within them. God rebuild within them a defense that's based on Scripture that they trust You, understand their spiritual authority as a daughter, as a son of the King of the Lord, our Savior. Fill them up with God with peace and healing grace. Displace all darkness and let life come. Keep them in your perfect peace. Lord, establish them in the night season and bring rest. God, no more sleepless nights. No more tormented nights, no more tossing and turning. Send the heavenly hosts God to guard and watch over them. Position their angels God as they sleep and have victorious dreams. God, we thank You, and we offer the body, the blood, the soul, we offer it all up to You. Lord, we thank You. In the name of Jesus, we have made our declaration. We have decreed a thing. We prophesied over a thing. **And it is so in Jesus' name! Halleluiah!**

God has promised you great things. I speak His blessing upon you all.
Walk into your freedom!

Dr. Shirley R Brown, Th.D.

Key Takeaways:

www.ingramcontent.com/pod-product-compliance
Lightning Source LLC
Chambersburg PA
CBHW081418080526
44589CB00016B/2588